SAINT AUGUSTINE

SAINT AUGUSTINE

THE ODYSSEY OF HIS SOUL

BY

KARL ADAM

TRANSLATED BY DOM JUSTIN MC CANN

LONDON
SHEED AND WARD
MCMXXXII

PERMISSU SUPERIORUM O.S.B.
NIHIL OBSTAT: INNOCENTIUS APAP, S. TH. M., O.P.
CENSOR DEPUTATUS.
IMPRIMATUR: ✠ JOSEPH BUTT,
VIC. GEN.
WESTMONASTERII, DIE 28º JANUARII, 1932

PRINTED IN GREAT BRITAIN
BY THE BURLEIGH PRESS
LEWIN'S MEAD, BRISTOL
FOR SHEED AND WARD
31 PATERNOSTER ROW
LONDON, E.C.4
FIRST PUBLISHED MARCH, 1932

PUBLISHER'S NOTE

THIS book is the translation of a centenary Address entitled *Die geistige Entwicklung des heiligen Augustinus*, delivered in the University of Tübingen at the celebrations in honour of St. Augustine held by the Catholic Theological Faculty on St. Monica's Day, May 4th, 1930, and repeated in the same year at the similar celebrations held in Munich (November 4th) and Cologne (December 3rd) by the Catholic University Union (*der Katholische Akademikerverband*).

The original was published in Germany in 1931, for the Catholic University Union, by Messrs. Haas and Grabherr of Augsburg.

v

SAINT AUGUSTINE

SAINT AUGUSTINE

AUGUSTINE is one of that small number of great minds who attract not merely the scientific study, but also the personal interest of the modern man. One reason for this is that his full life was lived at an important and even decisive turning-point of the history of the West. Son of a pagan father and Christian mother, he embodies in his own person that disturbed, uneasy period when paganism and Christianity were engaged in the final conflict. In his boyhood rang out the battle-cry of Julian the Apostate, who with a last desperate exercise of force would have wrested the Roman Empire from Christ and restored it to the heathen gods. When he had reached full manhood Augustine was a witness of that pregnant course of events in which Theodosius the Great established the Catholic Church, and bound together for better and for worse the fortunes of Christianity and the Empire, of Bishop and Emperor. And when Augustine came to old age, he saw the division between East Rome and West Rome, and so in a certain sense the birth of the West. Alaric had already appeared before Rome and the Teutonic tribes were busy destroying the Western Empire and building their own kingdoms out of its ruins. Finally, when he lay fever-stricken on his death-bed, he might have seen with his own eyes some of these representatives of the new world of the future, for the Vandals were besieging his episcopal city. Thus was Augustine, as regards his external life, a man of the transitional period. He stood with watchful eye upon the threshold of a new epoch, in which paganism was overcome by Christianity, the Empire by the barbarians, and when the first outlines of the West that was to be were beginning to be traced upon the sky of history.

But, besides the special character of the period in which he lived, the personality of St. Augustine wins our sympathy. In his *Confessions*, which were read with avidity in his own lifetime,[1] he narrates the history of his soul with a rare skill and exactitude, setting

forth the most complicated and obscure
processes in their native freshness and fra-
grance. It is a mirror in which we see
ourselves and our own experience. For
however much Augustine owes to the
spirit of his own time, that is to say,
to the spirit of the dying ancient world,
he is in the essentials of his mind a modern
man, modern beyond all else in his interest in
the phenomena of the inward life. In remarkable contrast to the attitude of the antique
man, who with a naive acceptance of his
own inner life boldly transcended its mysteries
and gave himself wholly to the external
world, Augustine turns inwards and finds
his first and truest interest in the observation
and study of the human soul. To that extent
Augustine is a conscious and deliberate em-
piricist. With extraordinary delicacy and
exactitude, with a truly " physiological
psychology,"[2] he describes, from his own
and others' experience, the phenomena,
functions and laws of the soul's life. His
description of the mind of the child, of its
joy and sorrow and untruth, his psychology
of compassion and of tragedy, of beauty and

3

of love, belong still in our own day to the best
that has been written upon those matters.
It is his habit thus to base himself upon
ascertained facts of consciousness and from
them to advance to the solid ground of reality.[3]
He discovers in man the presupposition of a
supreme truth, goodness and beauty, and from
that basis advances with sure step to the
reality of God. Over and over again he
makes psychological observation the preliminary and basis of metaphysic. And he
even ventures to apply his psychological
method to the deep mysteries of the divine
life, and to interpret the inner life of the
Trinity after the analogy of the life of the
human soul.

This empirical and psychological habit of
mind gives to his investigations that reality,
that concrete and lucid quality, and also that
quickening power which we feel to be
specifically Augustinian. On the other hand it
preserves his thought from eccentricities,
and however high the flights he may take,
he is never under any illusion regarding the
imperfections and limitations of human knowledge, not excepting the knowledge of the

theologian. It is no mere accident that it was Augustine who coined the phrase, *docta ignorantia* (learned ignorance).[4]

Among the great theologians, Augustine is pre-eminently the psychologist. In his psychological gift is rooted also his happy power of intuition, his faculty for tracking out the ultimate possibilities and implications of a doctrine by a certain prevision and instinct for the truth. There is scarcely a region of theology where he has not broken new ground, or at least has set out problems in the solution of which the centuries have toiled and we are still toiling.

On the other hand it is characteristic of this fresh, creative fertility of his psychological habit of mind that he neglected the purely logical relations and interconnections of the data which he had acquired, and did not seek to devise any neat and systematic arrangement of his thought. His philosophical and theological views tend to lie unconnected, in a relation of mere juxtaposition one to another. He does not contrive, or does not adequately contrive, to put them together in a higher synthesis and to give to each doctrine its proper place in the total fabric of his thought. Hence the fact that scholars are still uncertain about several of his opinions, and that there is scarcely any Christian sect which cannot appeal with some justification to his authority.

Augustine thinks and investigates as a living man, as one who in the first instance takes his problems from his own inner self, and who when a problem comes to him from without, refuses ever to regard it in mere isolation, always bringing it into relation with himself. To that extent is his theology a theology of experience. But it is emphatically not such in the sense that sacred things and divine truth had no existence for him except as objects of experience or facts of consciousness. He believed in absolute truth and in an absolutely valid knowledge, but he would bring these things into relation with himself, and they were for him living and fruitful only through that relation.

How far in this is Augustine from St. Thomas! To the mind of St. Thomas, the subject thinking, the theologian, is utterly subordinate to the object thought, to the sublime reality of revealed truth. To be a

theologian means for St. Thomas to receive
and interpret the word of God, and that alone,
in silent reverence. Beyond all subjectivity,
in inviolable security from every influence
or feeling or consideration, whether personal
or cultural, the truth in itself, the word of God
in itself, must be expounded in all its purity
and fulness. The only emotion that colours
the procedure of St. Thomas is that of an
answering service and single-minded devotion
to the word of God. This rejection of all
subjectivity gives St. Thomas's teaching its
supra-temporal character, its absolute validity,
its stability and permanence, but it gives it
at the same time a certain cold, rigid, and
impersonal quality. Augustine's theology, on
the other hand, cannot be separated from his
person and his time, and for that reason
contains a good deal that possesses only a
relative validity. But for the same reason
it has a quickening and kindling quality,
and has preserved that quality down to our
own days.

If Augustine, because of his psychological
habit of mind, is very near to the modern man,
nearer than any of the great scholastics : he

is still more modern in his life, that is to say in the special manner in which he lived his life, in its special rhythm and quality.

When his eyes began to open to the problems of life, Augustine did not belong to the communion of the Catholic Church. His devout mother, St. Monica, had from his infancy instilled the love of God and Christ into his heart, but Augustine had not received baptism or any solid Christian education. So he grew up in a state of religious isolation. The heritage which came to him from his pagan father—an unrestrained enjoyment of life, unlimited ambition, and a vivacious intelligence—naturally influenced him at first more powerfully than his mother's gift of a gentle disposition, a fine nobility of soul and a true piety. So he gave himself up, with all the zest of his passionate nature, to the pleasures of this world, to the pursuit of external glory and recognition, above all to the charms of love. " What was it that gave me pleasure, save to love and to be loved ? "[5] He was a pagan. " I was utterly empty . . . my soul was sick and sore, and threw itself into the external world."[6]

But even as a pagan he could not disown his mother. He was more restrained than his fellows. And he could not give his love where he found no spiritual response.[7] He was faithful to his mother's heritage above all in the very womanly delicacy with which he made and kept his friends. This need for intimacy with like-minded souls accompanied him his whole life through, and provided later on the natural basis upon which was built his theology of love and fellowship.

But his maternal heritage, bedewed by her prayers and tears, was presently to come to a far richer development. He read Cicero's *Hortensius*, in praise of philosophy, and " with a strange and heartfelt passion began to long for the immortality of wisdom." The book drove him, " not to run after this school or that, but to love and seek and pursue and clasp and never let go Wisdom herself, wherever I found her."[8] " O Truth, Truth, how did the inmost marrow of my soul sigh for thee even then."[9] Herein is manifested the very heart of Augustine, the passionate searcher for truth, struggling after the ultimate meaning of life, wrestling with God. For

9

that was his aim. Not content with the axioms and doctrines of any special science, nor content to investigate one special piece of reality, he must needs press onward to the foundations of all knowledge, to the invisible source and origin of all reality. And he held this aim for no mere scientific purpose, but for an intensely practical one. In seeking truth he was seeking the life of his life. Truth and happiness, *veritas* and *beata vita*, were to him one and the selfsame thing. All his searching and all his thinking came forth out of the depths of his personal life ; they were a deeply practical searching and thinking.

Let us come closer to our subject and ask what was the particular problem that stirred Augustine's soul. In order that we may not see his whole subsequent development in a false light, we must here at once lay it down that it was no question of the existence of God or of the Redemption by Christ. As he himself tells us repeatedly, he had from the start a living faith in God.[10] He got that from his mother. Moreover, Augustine was from the beginning in some sense, even if a superficial one, a believer in Christ. That too he got from his mother. It was, for instance, a grievous sorrow to him that Cicero's *Hortensius*, which so stirred his enthusiasm, lacked all mention of the name of Christ. And it was by this very test that he afterwards tried all the philosophies that came before him to ask his allegiance.[11] When he turned to the Manichæans the lure that drew him was "made up of the syllables of thy name and that of our Lord Jesus Christ."[12] And when he turned away from them, it was because he saw that their teaching lacked "the savour of Christ." The philosophers were just as little able to hold him, "for they were without the saving name of Christ."[13] We may fairly say that Augustine was already, in sentiment if not in conviction, far more a Christian than he himself was prepared to admit.

With what then was his passionate search for truth concerned? With the clearing up of certain difficulties and contradictions in which his conception of God was intolerably involved. At that period of his life, under the influence of popular stoicism, he could conceive of no reality which was not somehow material.

He was therefore faced with the problem:
How, considering the materiality of all being,
are we to think of God's being? Did God
exist in infinite material extension, like an
enormous sponge that has absorbed into itself
all that is not God? In any case it was clear
to him that God could not be conceived in
human form. And so he was very indignant
against the Church, for he supposed that the
Church encouraged such an anthropomorphic
conception of God, and for that reason
clung to the Old Testament where anthropo-
morphism was rampant. Thus he was
preoccupied and harassed by the search for a
tolerable and self-consistent conception of
God; and his search was accompanied with
hostility to the Church. Besides this problem
regarding God there was that other problem
of the origin of evil: How are evil, sickness,
sin and death to be reconciled with the
existence of God? According to his
materialistic presuppositions, evil also was a
material thing, a material substance. Could
the good God have made it? Was it not more
likely to be the work of an evil demon. And
here again there was antagonism to the

Church. For the Catholic Church, with the whole emphasis of her authority, ascribed moral evil, sin, to the free will of man. And the Church derived even physical evil, such as sickness and death, at least mediately, from the misuse of free will, from Adam's sin. As Augustine then stood, with senses very active and passions keenly alive, the Church's solution was bound to rouse in him the sharpest antagonism. How could man in his creaturely impotence himself produce evil, if evil be a material substantial thing? And in his moral nature the revolt against the Church was, if possible, even more violent. For he could not and would not give up that which the Church called evil. So this problem of evil fed his hostility to the Church with continually new fuel. And the fact that the Church, in this and in similar problems, gave no precise proof for her solution, but always threw into the scales the weight of her divine authority, filled his soul brimful with vexation. Did not this Catholic reliance on authority signify a gagging of free enquiry and a muzzling of the truth?

So it seemed clear to Augustine that if he

was to find the truth he must seek it by another road than that indicated by the Church. He must pursue his enquiry without the Church and against the Church.

And yet the very fact that Augustine took up this attitude of protest against the Church, striving constantly to contrast his views with the Church's doctrine and to show her wrong, betrays to the psychologist that the authority of the Church was already more deeply rooted in his subconsciousness than was apparent to his conscious mind. He fought against the Church because he had inwardly to fight against her, because she already stood in his soul as a challenging power and compelled him to conceive his struggle for truth as ultimately a struggle with the Catholic Church. The mother's influence was astir in her son.

But the son still fought against his mother. At the age of nineteen Augustine went over to the Manichees. He supposed that he would find among them the solution of his problems. Like the gnostics from whom they had sprung, the Manichæans rejected the Old Testament with its supposedly crude conception of God. They based their teaching regarding God and Christ upon seemingly scientific, astrological arguments. They spoke continually of truth,[14] appealed to the right of free enquiry, and rejected all faith as credulity. Furthermore, they explained sin and evil, not as a misdeed of one's own will, but as the product of an evil principle that was in conflict with the God of light. Thus all the requirements of his critical thought seemed to be satisfied, and, the most important point of all, his right to life and to a life full of sensual enjoyment, seemed secured. While Augustine for nine long years gave himself up to this crude Eastern dualism, he reached the extreme point of his revolt against his mother and of his divorce from the Church.

And yet the deepest yearnings of his soul remained unsatisfied. His love for truth was too sincere to allow him to befool himself permanently with the astrological lore of the Manichees and their " elegant cup-bearer " Faustus.[15] And—the decisive point—their teaching lacked the savour of Christ.[16] Then came a study of the Aristotelian and sceptical systems which shook the foundations of his Manichæanism. In this mood, thoroughly disturbed by doubts, he received his call to Milan as professor of rhetoric in the year 384.

At Milan, the preaching of its cultured, wise and devout bishop, St. Ambrose, first brought Augustine to a state of extreme doubt and despondency, and then became a determining influence in the crisis of his conversion. He now perceived that his condemnation of the Catholic doctrine of God and faith had been the result of misconception and rash judgment. But the most important thing of all was that, unknown to himself, under the influences that surrounded him, the Catholic faith in our Lord and Saviour won its way into his soul.[17] From day to day he absorbed it more and more deeply. He was overborne by the Christ of the Catholic Church as he began to know Him in Milan. But here too we may again trace his old heritage from his mother, the picture of Christ which Monica had imprinted upon his young soul. His childhood's lessons had prepared the way for the expositions of St. Ambrose and they made the Church's claim to authority more palatable to him. He found himself presently driven to the resolution: "I will plant my feet firmly on that ground where my parents placed me."[18]

But the two great problems were still unsolved, the problems which had troubled him from the start and brought him into conflict with the Church, viz., the problem of the true concept of God and the problem of the origin of evil. As we have seen, they were rooted in his materialistic presupposition that all existence must be corporeal, so that even God and evil must somehow or other be conceived as material substances.[19] The hopeless attempt to explain Christianity on a materialistic basis thrust him into an intolerable conflict. He became a victim of complete confusion of mind and unspeakable melancholy.

Augustine at this period of his life is a Faust-like figure. Between him and Goethe's Faust, as has been justly observed, there are many points of contact. In both there is the same passionate struggle for truth and for happiness of soul. In both an important part is played by astrology and demonism, by woman's love and worldliness. In both there is a despair of truth and a longing for death. And—to pass quickly to the end—in both is the same salvation through the "revelation of love that unfolds into blessedness."

From out of this wretchedness of his soul's conflict and oppression, from out of the misery of his materialistic philosophy, he was redeemed by a second great experience, the reading of Neoplatonist writings. In no philosophical system of antiquity was the spiritual so completely recognised and so wholeheartedly affirmed in its own nature and absolute self-sufficiency as in the system of Plato and his followers. The deeper Augustine penetrated into the Neoplatonic books—chiefly the *Enneads* of Plotinus—so much the more clearly did he realise the existence and reality of pure spirit, the existence of a spiritual world of ideas which is unchangeable, universally valid and necessary, and which therefore possesses a deeper and truer being than that possessed by transient, visible things. That was the knowledge which freed him and banished all doubt. He realised that there was being which was incorporeal and yet was superior to material being, that there was purely spiritual being. His materialistic thinking was thus conquered by idealism. The rest followed as a matter of course. God, the basis of the immutable ideal-world, was seen to be pure spirit. The human soul too, as organ and conveyer of the immutable ideas, was likewise purely spiritual. So Augustine had now, so to speak, discovered the region in which God and the soul have their eternal reality without any conflict with material being. He could now think of God and the soul without being terrified by the problem of space and extension. And at the same time that second question, of the origin of evil, was also solved. Since God as the absolute truth and absolute reality is the fulness of being, is immutable, true being, therefore that which is not God, which is in antagonism to God, such as sin and evil, is not material nor even anything existent at all, but essentially lack of being and a falling away from being.[20]

So was Augustine delivered from the oppression of his problems. His materialistic thinking had been overborne, and with it went his material conception of God and his dualistic cosmology. He was thus constrained to adopt an entirely new mental attitude. He was forced to realise that the mystery of being lay within, in his soul, and not without. "Go not out! Turn inwards into yourself! Truth dwells within, in the inward man." [21] Truth is to be found where God touches the soul. From this time forward the saint's thought swings constantly between these two poles, God and the soul. "I desire to know God and the soul. I desire nothing else."[22] Augustine turns back into himself, into the stillness of his heart, into the great silence. Augustine becomes a mystic.

It is very significant that when delivered from his materialism, Augustine without more ado recognised Catholic Christianity as the true Christianity. In itself, of course, the break through to idealism did not necessarily involve the acceptance of the Catholic Church. But it did for Augustine. And that fact is a further justification of our supposition that the Church and her authority had from the very start some sort of vitality in his subconsciousness. And so, as soon as all

the walls had fallen which he had built up
against her in his years of passion and conflict,
the Church stood out before him at once as
the one true Church. And for the same
reason also his deliverance from his old
prejudices was felt by him as a happy relief.[23]

But though it be certain that Augustine,
when he had attained the Neoplatonic concept
of spirit, was convinced without more ado of
the truth of the Church and its teaching, it
is equally certain that he saw the Church with
Neoplatonic eyes. His profession of faith
in the Catholic Church certainly included a
definite assent to all her dogma and discipline.
Augustine was certainly in conviction a full
and complete Catholic, and so he remained
to the end. But he saw Catholicism at that
time in a Neoplatonic light. Or rather, he
then identified Christianity in essentials with
Neoplatonism, for he took account only of
what was common to the two, and not of
their points of difference and opposition.
Among their points of agreement he fastened
especially on the conception of God as pure
spirit. Augustine took over the Neoplatonic
teaching regarding the divine spirit, without

at that time perceiving its pantheistic implications.

The God of Neoplatonism did indeed
stand beyond all changing, corporeal, sensible
things, and in essential contrast to them.
But he did not stand beyond spirit itself. He
was not absolutely transcendent, the creative
source of spirit and non-spirit alike. He was
rather the apex and summit of spiritual being;
and being in himself infinitely fruitful, radiated
spiritual force, by descending degrees, into
the universe. That force flowed into men,
and so effectively that man's soul, as a fragment
of that divine spiritual power, might by regular
degrees raise itself up to the divine spirit
and become one with it in ecstatic contemplation. Augustine himself believed that he
had thus touched the divine spirit "in the
flash of one trembling glance."[24] The
Neoplatonists taught that the divine stood
in essential union with all spirit and in essential
opposition to all non-spirit. That being their
theory, morality necessarily meant the morti-
fication of the body and its senses in order to
free the spirit, that spark of divine life, from
the grip of the sensible and prepare it for

union with the supreme spirit. The aim of Neoplatonic ethics was not the transformation of sense, but its destruction.

It is a specially tragic circumstance in the history of this great saint that at the moment when Neoplatonism had taught him the reality of spirit, he should have been delivered up by this same Neoplatonism to an exaggerated spiritualism.

Nothing proves this more plainly than the further history of his conversion. It was because Augustine was seeing Christianity in a Neoplatonic light, that he believed that in order to become a Christian he would have to trample on his sensual nature. His soul was too delicate and conscientious for him to venture to offer himself for baptism, before he felt sure that he could mortify his sensual life. So there began for this sensually-keen, passionate nature a fearful and formidable struggle, a struggle against the body and all its works. Above all it was a struggle against woman. He who had thought it wretchedness to be deprived of a woman's embrace,[25] now regarded it as his conscientious duty to renounce every form of such love, and even marriage itself. This renunciation then appeared to him to be not only an evangelical counsel and expression of a special effort after perfection, but as a moral duty required by his new ethical attitude towards the sensual life. The gnostic condemnation of the flesh as a corrupting principle—which view he had got from the Manichees—was not corrected by Neoplatonism, but rather confirmed. And so Augustine believed that even marriage involved a certain sensual contamination,[26] however ready he was to recognise the value of a well-ordered family life and the careful upbringing of children.[27] Therefore he declined to enter upon the married state, though his prudent mother had counselled that course. His conscience was too sensitive to allow him to compromise in this matter, and in the mental state he was then in marriage seemed to be a compromise. So there, was a fierce struggle. " There were two wills in me, the old and the new, the carnal and the spiritual, and they were in conflict, and their discord paralysed my soul."[28] The astonishing news of the conversion of the distinguished rhetorician Victorinus, and the affecting history of the severely penitential life of Antony and his disciples, drove him more and more towards the decisive refusal of the life of the senses, even though the carnal man should wilt and break under the strain. And finally, when the inward conflict had reached its acutest point, when he was as one mad, when he raged against himself because he could not make that covenant with God for which all his bones cried out; then the voice and the words of a child made him turn to the Scriptures. And there as though with new eyes he read the words of the apostle of the gentiles: "Not in rioting and drunkenness, not in chambering and impurities, not in contention and envy: but put ye on the Lord Jesus Christ." As soon as he had read the passage "the light of peace seemed to be shed upon my heart and every shadow of doubt melted away."[29] Augustine was converted. It was in intention a conversion to Catholic Christianity, for Augustine wished to be nothing else than a completely Catholic Christian, but the conversion was consummated in a Neoplatonic atmosphere. Assuredly

God, who sees the heart and the will, recognised the Christian soul despite its Neoplatonic garb and heard its cry for grace.

Considered in a purely psychological fashion, this break-through and victory of the spiritual man is certainly the final result of a long process of development. His childhood impressions of God, Christ and the Church lay on the margin of his conscious mind, or perhaps only in the subconsciousness. These impressions drew to themselves increasingly all related ones, especially the spiritual and moral doctrines of Neoplatonism, and heaped them up upon the margin of the field of consciousness. The larger became their mass, the stronger was its influence upon the experiences of his early manhood—very different these and even contradictory—which filled the centre of the field. Augustine felt the conflict of these rival experiences as a violent mental tension. This tension became continually more intolerable, the more his outward and inward experiences strengthened his spiritual aspirations. He became a prey to feelings of boundless self-depreciation, of unspeakable sadness and depression. In

the instant when Augustine in that garden
thought himself near to despair, the spiritual
experiences which had been amassed on the
margin of his consciousness got the upper
hand, broke suddenly into the middle of the
field, and all at once superseded the experiences
which he had been accumulating since his
youth. He felt like one suddenly new born,
and he could not interpret this transformation
in any other way than as an interposition of
supernatural force, an effect of grace.

So, if we consider it in this purely
psychological fashion, Augustine's conversion
is nothing but a triumphant re-assertion and
break-through, in the mature man, of the
religious impressions of his childhood.
Monica had won at last. There is no better
example anywhere of the enormous importance of the first religious impressions, that
is to say, of parental instruction, in the spiritual
growth of a man. And the chief factor which
released these pent-up forces was that body of
experiences and convictions which we have
designated as Neoplatonic.

But there would be no greater mistake
than to suppose that by such a purely

psychological analysis of Augustine's conversion we had exhaustively solved the problem which it presents. Psychology may describe the process of a conversion, but it can never explain it fundamentally. What that ultimate force was, which employing every physio-psychological law and working with definite aim and dogged perseverance, so governed the sequence of Augustine's experience that the sensual man was finally transformed into a spiritual man : which moving forward with that same definite purpose prevented any reversal of the process and protected him from relapse—the nature of that ultimate, purposive force will for ever remain out of reach of the psychologist. Here is the sphere of faith and of the theologian. And the theologian knows but this, that he must join with the man who felt the working of this ineffable force, and with him praise the mercy of God and glorify his grace.

The fact that Augustine's conversion was a completely sincere conversion to Catholic Christianity and yet was accomplished by the bridge of Neoplatonism must be kept very steadily in view in what follows, while we endeavour to portray his mental development as a Christian. It was precisely the vigorous Neoplatonic elements remaining embedded in his mind that provided the stimulus for his full theological development, so much so, that we can regard his whole subsequent evolution as a progressive deliverance from Neoplatonism and a growth into essential Christianity. Augustine would scarcely have become the great saint that he did, and certainly not the great theologian, had not his own development forced him into a continual argument with Neoplatonism.

Nowhere is this inward struggle plainer than in his effort towards a comprehensive statement of Christianity, when he sets himself to the task of discovering the essential nature of the new thing which he had received in baptism and of relating it to the old, that is to say in the question of questions, What is Christianity?

We have emphasized the point that Augustine from childhood to youth and throughout the stormy period of his early manhood, clung at least in feeling and sentiment to our Lord and Saviour. Even as a Manichee he professed his belief in "Our Saviour, the only begotten Son of God," without being able of course, because of his gnostic prejudices, to believe in the true humanity of Jesus.[30] After his break with the Manichees he was still unable to achieve a deep understanding of the mystery of the Incarnation, yet he honoured Christ as a "man of surpassing wisdom and without rival."[31] When he entered the Church he took over her faith in the Incarnate God, and he took it over completely without any limitation. When his friends at Cassicium suggested that perhaps the Father only should be called God in the full sense of that word, he corrected them very emphatically[32]. At no point in the whole of his subsequent history can we say that he held anything less than the full faith that Christ is true God and true man.

In this basic belief, then, that Christ is at once God and man, that there is no Christianity without the Incarnate God, Augustine after his conversion never wavered. But he did undergo a change of view in regard to the functions which should be ascribed respectively to the divinity of Christ and his humanity in the inauguration and building up of the Christian life. It is important to notice that the different and even contradictory answers which Augustine gave to this question were conditioned by his changing attitude towards Neoplatonism. The critical point was this : Am I redeemed because Christ is the divine Truth itself, or because he became my human Brother ? Is redemption a deliverance from error through the Word of God, or a deliverance from sin through the servant of God ? In his early period Augustine favoured the first solution ; in his later, maturer period the second. In the sequel his whole theology took from this second solution its special character.

The first line of demarcation in his Christian career may be drawn at the year 391 when he was ordained to the priesthood. While he was as yet not a priest, i.e., from 387 to 391, Augustine was dominated by the mental mood in which his conversion had been effected. He was determined to be a full and perfect Christian, but he still saw Christianity with Neoplatonic eyes. He had not yet penetrated into its depths, and therefore was able to suppose that Platonism and Christianity were not essentially different. Had Plato but known the deep transforming power of Catholicism, he would have had to change "only a few words and phrases" in his philosophy in order to become a Christian.[33]

So Augustine at this period interprets the mystery of Christ in a Neoplatonic fashion. Christ is the true Son of God, the Word, Truth, Wisdom and Power of God. So far as the terminology goes Augustine is in accord with the Church's teaching; but it is different when we examine the content of his terms. For he identified the Word and Wisdom of God with the "paternal mind" (πατρικὸς νοῦς) of the Neoplatonists, that ultimate divine force which radiating from the One contains in itself the patterns and essences of all things and creatively produces them. Christ, the Son of God, is identical with that ultimate truth in which all the essences of things are based and whence they get their existence. He is therefore the measure, archetype and ultimate exemplar of the created world.[34]

Augustine was of course too genuine a Christian to share the pantheism which lies at the bottom of these Neoplatonic conceptions. He is sure of the Son's essential likeness with the Father; he is sure that he did not proceed from the Father in some eternal cosmic process, but that he was born from him from all eternity. And furthermore he is quite sure of this, that things have not come forth from the creative word by some inner natural necessity, but are the creatures of his free creative will.

On those points, therefore, Augustine forces the Neoplatonic logos-doctrine into a Christian mould; but he remains a Neoplatonist in his view that to be a Christian is to know the Son. And to know the Son means nothing else than an immediate contemplation of the immutable truths that are pre-supposed in and given with the eternal divine truth.[35] Christianity becomes a contemplative mysticism, a grasping of all immutable truth in the truth which is Christ. Through this immediate contemplation we attain to union with God himself, and even to union with the Triune God, so far as that is here possible.[36] Augustine at this period of his life regards it as quite possible that certain elect souls should even on earth have this immediate vision of the Trinity, not of course at once, but after a methodical ascent by seven degrees from sensible things to the supra-sensible Godhead.[37]   Christianity is therefore identical with true philosophy and is essentially an intellectual activity.[38]   Beatitude also consists in nought else but an eternal experience of truth.[39]

Augustine thus regards Christianity, after the Greek fashion, from a purely intellectual standpoint.   The true Christian is the philosopher (*sapiens*) who adheres steadfastly to the truth and never swerves from the right judgement (*recta ratio*).   True virtue consists in this right judgement, and in so far as the philosopher holds it, he can never sin.[40]

Regarded from the standpoint of this theory the mediatorship of Christ lies exclusively in his divinity.   For it is only because Christ is God that he is the eternal Word, Truth, and Wisdom which inwardly liberates and enlightens our souls.[41]   Hence the fundamental word in Christianity is not faith, but knowledge.   Faith is not a saving act, but only a sort of substitute for knowledge, a

34

substitute which the sensual, carnal man must employ until he has been made capable of the immediate contemplation of truth. This obviously is an extreme hellenization of Christianity. Just as Augustine, in his Manichæan period, had interpreted Christianity in terms of materialism, so now (under the spell of Neoplatonism) he seeks to hellenize it.

Since redemption is wrought by the divinity of Christ, by Christ as the eternal Word and eternal Truth, therefore his humanity has only a subordinate importance in the business of our salvation. In order to define its function more precisely, Augustine again appealed to Neoplatonism, in particular to its doctrine that only *he* can see the immutable truth who has cleansed his heart and purged it of all sensual desire. But whereas the Neoplatonists were content to leave this business of purification to man's moral idealism Augustine took a different path. He knew that the sensual man necessarily fails at this point, unless the moral ideal, the *auctoritas divini intellectus*, is visibly brought before him in the person of the Incarnate God and summons him to imitation.[42] The Christian is

35

distinct from the Neoplatonist precisely in this that he directs his gaze, not upon himself, but upon the Incarnate Son of God, from whose lowliness (*humilitas*) he learns to know his own pride and to put it away. So the whole gist of the Incarnation is this, that it indicates man's special vocation to eternal truth, that it sets the divine laws before us in the person of Christ in their "compelling majesty and radiant clearness," and finally that it gives human striving its true exemplar and model (*exemplum vivendi*).[43] The death also of Christ and his resurrection find their true meaning in their power to inspire and guide the believer. When Christ died the death of the cross and rose again to new life, he showed us that in the pursuit of wisdom no obstacle is insurmountable, and that we need fear no manner of death.[44]

Obviously Augustine is still too much a Neoplatonist to ascribe a genuine redeeming power to Christ's Incarnation, Death and Resurrection, and to set them in the heart and centre of Christianity. He is silent about the Lamb that taketh away the sins of the world, just as he has nothing to say at this period

concerning sorrow or penance for past sins.
All that man has to do is, imitating Christ,
to purge his heart of all ignoble affections and
to prepare it for the immediate contemplation
of eternal truth in the divine Word. And it
is this contemplation that redeems and sanctifies
us.

Augustine himself may have felt that in
this conception of Christianity he had got
very far away from its true nature, as understood by St. Paul, St. John and the Catholic
Church. That would explain the passionate
insistence with which he implored Bishop
Valerian, when in 391 he found himself constrained to be a priest, to give him a respite
until Easter so that he might work his way
right through the Scriptures.[45]

Of course I do not say that we should regard
this intensive study of the Scriptures as the
definite starting-point of an entirely new stage
in his evolution. Augustine's thought was
so personal and so integral, that the transition
to the new was not abrupt but gradual, and
at almost every stage could be linked up with
what had gone before. He had no hesitation
in holding on still to those Neoplatonic

expressions which admitted of a Christian interpretation. He did not now break completely with Neoplatonism. As long as he lived he extolled it for this its special achievement, that it had recognised and proclaimed the immutability of eternal truth.[46]

But the study of the Scriptures opened his eyes and he now saw in Neoplatonism not only what it had in common with Christianity, but also the points in which it was essentially different. Among these latter points were in particular its monistic conception of God as immanent in the world, and its general intellectualistic attitude. Such was Augustine's new judgement, to which he now gave explicit expression and to which he returned later in express criticism of his own earlier attitude : " To live happily is not only to live according to reason, for that would be to live according to a human standard. To live happily is to live according to the mind of God."[47] Instead of the immanence of God we now hear of his transcendence. The antitheses with which Christianity is concerned are not of this world. It is not concerned with the contrast of sensual and spiritual, flesh and spirit, sensible and spiritual world ;[48] but rather with the contrast of this world and the next, of time and eternity, of the kingdom of the world and the kingdom of God. So we have not to avoid the corporeal and the sensible because they are such, but to avoid the misuse of sense and spirit alike.[49] The measure and test of all morality and all holiness is the inward surrender and complete orientation of the soul to God. Where there is no such orientation and a man finds his end in himself, even in his spiritual self, there his fairest virtues are " vices rather than virtues."[50] And so the fundamental activity of Christianity is not a proud knowledge but a humble faith, the humble acceptance by man of that wisdom of God which to the world is foolishness. Faith is no longer a mere preliminary to knowledge, but has its own independent value. It is a function of salvation. And this faith is essentially an act of will, a decision, and an initial love.[51] So the chief place is now occupied, not by knowledge, but by an earnest inward acceptance and performance of the will of God. Augustine has passed from an intellectualist into a voluntarist. The true Christian is no

longer the philosopher, but the man who is
striving to become spiritual (*spiritalis*).   Truth
is no longer the highest and ultimate thing,
but charity.   Or rather genuine truth is
based on charity and passes into charity.   He
had already celebrated the praises of charity,
as the basic quality of the Christian, in his
treatise on the *Morals of the Catholic Church*
which was completed in 390.   From now on,
with ever deeper understanding of the spirit
of the New Testament, he repeats and repeats
the sentence of the apostle of the gentiles :
" The charity of God is poured forth in our
hearts by the Holy Spirit who is given us."
Love is the deepest reality of all, for God is
love.   It is the motive-power of the Christian[52]
and it gives its right value to all his doing.
" Love and do what you will."[53]   Love
alone differentiates the true Christian from the
seeming Christian.   " Anyone may sign himself with the sign of the cross, may say ' Amen '
and sing ' Alleluia,' may present himself for
baptism, visit churches and help to build
them.   The only thing which distinguishes
the children of God from the children of
the devil is love."[54]   That great canticle of

love which St. Paul had sung is re-echoed by
Augustine and by him enthusiastically com-
mended to succeeding centuries. It would
be hard to find a Father or a theologian who
shows such inward appreciation of it as does
this bishop of the glowing heart, St. Augustine.
By a happy inspiration the artists of the Church
have depicted him with a flaming heart in
his hand.

But how may a man attain to this great and
holy love? Here is the point wherein
Augustine's change from Neoplatonic conceptions to a pure and complete Christianity
is most strikingly evident.

In the period of his priesthood he is quite
sure that love, that true substance of the new
life in God, is effected in the soul by God, is a
work of the Holy Spirit. And indeed even
the Neoplatonists taught that the new life
of the spirit was infused by the supreme
Spirit. So Augustine speaks of an " infusion "
of love. But at that period he is of the opinion
that faith, the basis of the new life of love, is
a work of the man himself. However
emphatically he spoke at that time of the
" mass of sin "⁵⁵ and however much he made

man's fate depend upon the mercy of God, yet he had no thought of a deep-seated corruption of human nature. He does not yet speak of a real hereditary guilt, but only of inherited ignorance and weakness of will. These two things dispose man to evil, yet he may by the strength and initiative of his own free-will, supported by God's grace, overcome all evil tendencies.[56] So human nature is not hopelessly corrupt and therefore it can of its own strength achieve at least the beginning of the new life, that is faith.[57] Thus at this period of his life, as he himself afterwards very candidly admitted,[58] he assessed man's condition in a relatively optimistic fashion. His views were in fact much the same as those of the Semipelagians later. Human nature, in spite of all sin, has a kernel untouched by sin, a sound will, with which the Christian can make his act of faith. It is clear that the old leaven of his Neoplatonism was still alive in him ; he had a robust confidence in his own native strength.

Then came the year 396 and Augustine was consecrated bishop. The troublous experiences of his pastoral work, the moral deficiencies of clergy and monks, and not least of all his own conscientious self-scrutiny had long destroyed that cheerful optimism which had supposed that it was possible even in this life to contemplate the Trinity. And the same experiences had already taught him the saving value of sorrow for sin and penance. With these experiences to his credit, and in order that he might answer a friend's questions, he made in 397 a fresh study of St. Paul's epistles, in particular of the Epistles to the Romans and Galatians. As a result he reached the clear conviction that faith too was a gift of God's grace, [59] and was in effect the first manifestation of the mercy of God towards his creature. He saw now with amazement the full meaning of the Scripture words: "What hast thou, man, that thou hast not received?" Later on, in his controversy with the Semipelagians, he elaboratd fully this fundamental point. His conclusion was that our human nature has absolutely nothing in itself which of itself, by its purely natural value, is fit for the Kingdom of God. Adam's sin has affected not only our personal activity, our knowing and willing, but also our very nature. Mankind is a mass of sin.[60]

It was only when he had attained this new outlook that Augustine succeeded in getting to the heart of the Christian doctrine of redemption and in expounding it fully. Since mankind is corrupted in its very nature, there is only one redemption possible, viz., that we should get a new nature by incorporation in a new and sinless humanity. We must acquire a completely new foundation and a new root. We need to find a new man, who though free from the curse of sin and united with God, is yet one of ourselves, bound to us by the bonds of a common blood and common life. Redemption became possible only when God graciously ordained that such a man should come down upon the earth and that his life should be our life, his death our death, his resurrection our resurrection. So Christianity is simply the good tidings of the new man and of our incorporation in him.[61] This new man is Christ. Being taken up into the creative Word of God, he is not a mere man as we are ; he is *the* man, the new Adam, the head of mankind, the basis and first-fruits of

44

the society of the redeemed[62]; he is the new
humanity itself. Just as the whole of mankind
was germinally contained in Adam, so is the
whole of the new, redeemed humanity, the
fellowship of the elect, contained in this second
Adam, because he is in his own person the
creative Word of God. Redeemed humanity
is to be regarded as an unfolding in space
and time of the humanity of Jesus.[63] Christ
is the head, we are his members. And therefore Christ is whole and entire only when head
and members are together. So intimate is
this fellowship of being and life that Augustine
does not hesitate to speak of Christ and his
members as one single Christ, and as one single
man.[64] This real, essential union of our
humanity with the new man, Christ, is the
sum and climax of Augustine's teaching
regarding the redemption. He no longer
considers the Incarnate Word alone. This
essential union with the new man is established
by the sacrament of baptism ; and the sacrament of the eucharist knits together the
Christian fellowship, joining man to man
until all the redeemed form but one single
person. Christianity is therefore essentially

sacramental, for it is by means of the sacraments that our union with Christ is established, renewed and deepened. In his early period Augustine had little use for the sacraments; he now sees in them the most speaking symbols and most perfect expression of Christianity. For the sacraments are exclusively concerned with the enactment of the central Christian "mystery," our essential union with the new man Christ.

No doubt Augustine propagated in this way a new understanding of St. Paul's profoundest thoughts, of the thoughts expressed in his "one mediator, the man Christ Jesus," and in his teaching regarding the new Adam, the first-born among many brethren, the Body of Christ, the Head and its members. Not that St. Paul's teaching had ever been wholly forgotten. Ignatius of Antioch, Ambrose, Ambrosiaster and Hilary all celebrate the mystery of the Body of Christ. Even a Donatist such as Tykonius undoubtedly conceived the Church as the one Body of Christ.[65] But no Father before Augustine, nor theologian after him, has treated this mystical unity so profoundly, or employed it so fruitfully and

comprehensively in expounding the essential
nature of Christianity and the Church. In this
Augustine was the inspired pupil of an inspired
master, the great apostle of the gentiles.
But Augustine—however astonishing this may
appear—owed his excellent understanding of
St. Paul to that very Neoplatonism which
he here vanquished with Pauline weapons.
For Neoplatonism beyond all other systems
had insisted on the unity of all spirit and its
essential solidarity with the divine. Augustine
rejects very decisively their view that the
soul is a part of God,[66] nor will he have anything to do later with his erstwhile risky
conception of the world as a living being
informed by one general soul[67] ; nevertheless
the fundamental Neoplatonic notion of the
oneness of all being seemed to him to be
illuminating, at least as an abstract theory.
By its means he certainly came to a better
understanding and appreciation of St. Paul's
doctrine of the unity of the mystical Body of
Christ, though this conception derived of
course from quite different premises. Even
before he was a priest Augustine had considered
the idea that mankind, from Adam to the last

man, might be regarded as one entity, as a single human life.[68]

But however that may be, it is quite certain that the real union of the members of Christ with their Head, our Incarnate Saviour, not only stands at the centre of Augustine's doctrine of the redemption, but is in the very heart of his theology. Grace and predestination occupied a large place in the interests of himself and his disciples; but they did not occupy the first place. The first place was taken by this his fundamental conception of Christianity as a vital union of all the redeemed with the new man who is Christ.

(is this not "grace")

But we should interpret Augustine wrongly, were we to see in his teaching on this point nothing but a modification of the so-called "recapitulation theory." According to this theory man's redemption was effected by the mysterious act of the Incarnation alone, for by this act we were in Christ re-united to God, and definitively re-united. Now it was Augustine's great achievement, on the contrary, that he did not conceive the union of mankind with the divine Word as a static thing, as an absolutely unitary mystical occur-

48

rence, but as a dynamic thing, working itself out continuously in the Incarnate Christ. The cause of redemption is not so much the Incarnation in its supra-historical meaning and value, as the Incarnate Person in his historical existence and activity, in his life, death and resurrection. When the Christian is incorporated in him by faith and love, he obtains a share in his life, death and resurrection. " He is the head, we are the body ; what he suffered in his own person, that we also have suffered in him."[69] Christ became man in order to offer for us the sacrifice of his Passion, the sacrifice of the Cross.[70] If Augustine does not define the redemptive act, in the manner of St. Anselm, as an atonement, yet he lays great emphasis on its being " for our sins," and a " sacrifice offered for us."[71] " Human nature can be justified in no other way than by faith and the sacrament of his death." " He died for our sins and rose again for our justification."[72] Augustine conceives the whole life of Jesus as a redeeming sacrifice. In order to elaborate this sacrificial quality, he employs almost all the theories of redemption that tradition offered, without expressly tying himself to any particular one. The essential point for him was the certainty that the Head of the Body lived and suffered, died and rose again for his members, and in that way redeemed them from the guilt of sin. The older he grew the more did Augustine cherish this conviction that this forgiveness of sin through Christ is the basis of our deepest and truest righteousness.[73]

But the redemptive activity of Christ is not confined to this work of atonement. The dynamic character of Augustine's view is especially plain in his doctrine that Christ manifests himself in his members as the continuous active principle of the new life. It is not the mere individual that believes in Christ, prays and loves, but Christ in him through his Holy Spirit, the Head in his members. And here Augustine adds his doctrine of grace and predestination. The new subject of faith and love is not the natural man, but the man incorporated in Christ. It is by the profound and inscrutable judgements of God, his fore-knowledge of his own unfathomable divine activity, and not by any prevision of mere human action,[74] that we must explain God's calling of his elect and his leading them by the way of faith and love. It is true that man has by nature a capacity for faith,[75] and therefore is able to concur with the impulse of grace.[76] Nevertheless it is the incalculable influences of divine grace that set his will in motion. Insinuating themselves into his higher spiritual striving, they attract the will by their sweetness,[77] redeem it from its bondage to sense, make it sound and free,[78] and so stimulate it to concurrence that the will gives itself to the truth with a free interior assent, unswervingly and invincibly.[79] So faith, in its radiant reality and vital fulness, is exclusively God's work.[80]

Therefore Christianity is essentially grace, the grace of the Incarnation of Christ unfolding itself in space and time. And humility and love are for Augustine the specifically Christian virtues. At this stage in his development his conception of those virtues becomes far wider. Humility ceases to be a mere subordination of self for the attainment of the truth, and love to be merely the service of our fellows; both obtain a universal scope. Since Christianity is essentially the grace of

God, therefore humility is the fundamental attitude of the Christian. " While we are on earth our perfection lies in humility."[81] It is a complete consciousness of our unlimited dependence upon God. And since Christianity is of its nature a union of Head and members in one body, so Christian love is love of the whole body, a social love in the most comprehensive sense. All Christendom is " one Christ, loving himself."[82] According to Augustine's mind, the true Christian is never alone, never solitary. He is conscious always of his union with Christ and his members. His sympathies are not confined and restricted, but go out always to the whole great fellowship.

And that of itself explains the important position held by the Church in Augustine's theology. According to Augustine there exists between the Church and the Body of Christ an identity, not indeed of external manifestation but of inward nature : the Church is the sole place wherein Christ works in his members through his Holy Spirit. So saints are possible only in the Church, and they do occur there, though there is unworthiness also. These saints, because they are impregnated with the Spirit of their head, are the fruitful source of the Church's grace, the treasure and support of the Church. There is no grace in the Church which is not somehow due to the communion of Saints. The visible distributors of grace are the officials of the Church, its "servants," who have their authority neither from themselves, nor from the faithful, but directly from Christ. Consequently the Church is the true and only home of salvation, the revelation and manifestation of Christ's saving power, the Body of Christ.

Augustine's identification of the Church with the Body of Christ is the basis of his teaching that the Church is the only home of salvation, and of his severity towards all schismatical and heretical communities. The older he grew, the less favourable was his judgement on them. In the end he went so far as to say that " outside the Church there is nothing but the damned,"[83] a proposition that was condemned by the Church at the time of the Jansenist controversy. On the same equation of the Church with the Body of Christ is based his triumphant faith in the

Church's future. Though the Roman Empire fall, though the barbarian destroy his episcopal city, though the citizens of the devil penetrate into the inmost sanctuary and desecrate the altars : yet the city of God will continue to live her vigorous life in the Church. The Church must and will conquer, because it is the Body of Christ.

We have reached the end. To be a man is to be a fighter, and that is pre-eminently true of Augustine. He is sure of a place among the great figures of history for the single reason that he was, as few have been, a seeker of the truth. He devoted his whole life, his mind and his body, to that most daring and most sublime of quests, the pursuit of the truth that saves. Nor did Augustine merely state the problem and give no answer. He had the courage to give an answer, even though the answer involved pain and conflict. It is this that gives a sublime quality to his whole life.

In estimating his importance in the history of thought, we must surely admit that it does not lie merely in his successful controversies

with the errors of his time and in the
consequent clarification and deepening of
momentous philosophical and theological ideas.
Much more important than this was his
influence on the interior life of the Church
and on Catholic piety. Augustine gave the
Christians of his day a new realization of their
faith, and to many almost discovered it anew.
Since the days when the apologists had fought
with Gnosticism there were certain groups
in the Church who understood Christianity
after a very formal fashion. It was a doctrine
and a discipline : a divine doctrine which
man must accept for his instruction, and a
divine discipline according to which he must
order his life. But Augustine, penetrating
deeply into the writings of St. Paul and of the
great Fathers, realized that Christianity was
more than this. He saw that it was essentially
a redemption, and that it was based essentially
on the mystery of the Incarnation. To be a
Christian is not merely to accept divine truth
and obey divine commands. To be a Christian
is to be born again of the Holy Ghost, to be
born again in the new man, who is Christ.
That is Augustine's glad tidings, the faith that

made his life strong and victorious, the joy
that rejoiced his heart : " Christ is my beginning, Christ is my root, Christ is my head."[84]
It is from this standpoint that he interprets
paganism and Christianity, God and the world.
Let us repeat what we have said before : there
is no Father of the Church and no theologian
who has expounded the essential nature of
the Church so profoundly and so lucidly as
Augustine. Nor has any expounded it with
such infectious power, such rich fulness of
experience and such a splendid eloquence.

In conclusion we may well ask ourselves
how we have treated Augustine's legacy.
Have we guarded the heart and centre of his
teaching with the care with which he
bequeathed it to us ? Are we true heirs of
his ? It is a searching question, nor is the
answer very comforting. Do we all really
know what it is to be redeemed ? Or is
Nietzsche's pointed saying true of vast numbers
of Christians ? " The redeemed must be yet
more redeemed." There is something profoundly lacking to our lives. Why have
egotism and self-seeking individualism been

able to strike root so deeply? And why have they produced among the poor and destitute that false and distorted idea of fellowship which is communism? It is because we have been and are superficial Christians. In particular it is because we have for centuries failed to appreciate those immense forces, powerful to create genuine fellowship and powerful to maintain it, which flow from Christianity such as Augustine taught it, from a living faith in the essential union of all Christians with one another and with Christ their Head, from the mystery of the Body of Christ. We need a renewal, a renewal from the ultimate source of our being, a re-birth in God. And such a re-birth must in large measure mean a revival of the spirit of Augustine and of Augustinian Christianity.

So Augustine's is no figure that merely stands out luminous in the dark and distant past. He is a beacon enlightening the path that lies before us, illuminating the future. With a new and sublime meaning may we say: Augustine is not dead, Augustine is living still.

NOTES

[1] Quid autem meorum opusculorum frequentius et delectabilius innotescere potuit quam libri confessionum mearum? (*De Dono Perseverantiae*, 20.)

[2] Cf. A. Harnack, *Reflexionen und Maximen*, xv.

[3] Nam et sumus et nos esse novimus et id esse ac nosse diligimus. In his autem tribus, quae dixi, nulla nos falsitas veri similis turbat. Non enim ea, sicut illa, quae foris sunt, ullo sensu corporis tangimus, velut colores videndo, sonos audiendo, odores olfaciendo, sapores gustando, dura et mollia contrectando sentimus, quorum sensibilium etiam imagines eis simillimas, nec jam corporeas, cogitatione versamus, memoria tenemus, et per ipsas in istorum desideria concitamur. Sed sine ulla phantasiarum vel phantasmatum imaginatione ludificatoria, mihi esse me, idque nosse et amare certissimum est. Nulla in his veris Academicorum argumenta formido, dicentium, quid si falleris? Si enim fallor, sum. Nam qui non est, utique nec falli potest, ac per hoc sum, si fallor. Quia ergo sum, si fallor, quomodo esse me fallor, quando certum est me esse, si fallor? (*De Civitate Dei*, XI, 26.)

[4] Est ergo in nobis quaedam, ut ita dicam, docta ignorantia, sed docta spiritu Dei, qui adjuvat infirmitatem nostram. (*Epistola* CXXX, 15.)

[5] Et quid erat, quod me delectabat, nisi amare et amari ? (*Confess.* II, 2.)

[6] *Ibid.*, III, 1.

[7] *Ibid.*

[8] *Ibid.*, III, 4.

[9] O veritas, veritas, quam intime etiam tum medullae animi mei suspirabant tibi. (*Ibid.*, III, 6.)

[10] Nulla pugnacitas calumniosarum quaestionum per tam multa quae legeram inter se confligentium philosophorum extorquere mihi potuit, ut aliquando non crederem te esse quidquid esses, quod ego nesciebam, aut administrationem rerum humanarum ad te pertinere. (*Ibid.*, VI, 5 ; cf. VII, 7 ; VII, 19.)

[11] Et hoc solum me in tanta flagrantia refrangebat, quod nomen Christi non erat ibi. (*Ibid.*, III, 4.) Quia nec sapiebas in ore meo sicuti es. (*Ibid.*, III, 6.)

[12] *Ibid.*, III, 6.

[13] Quibus tamen philosophis, quod sine nomine salutari Christi essent, curationem languoris animae meae committere omnino recusabam. (*Ibid.*, V, 14.)

[14] Dicebant " veritas et veritas " et multum eam dicebant mihi, et nusquam erat in eis. (*Ibid.*, III, 6.)

[15] Sed quid ad meam sitim pretiosorum poculorum decentissimus ministrator ? (*Ibid.*, V, 6.)

[16] *Ibid.*, III, 6.

[17] *Ibid.*, VII, 5.

[18] *Ibid.*, VI, 11.

[19] Et quoniam cum de Deo meo cogitare vellem, cogitare nisi moles corporum non noveram, neque enim videbatur mihi esse quidquam quod tale non

esset, ea maxima et prope sola causa erat inevitabilis
erroris mei. (*Ibid.*, v, 10.)

[20] Cf. *Contra Ep. Manichaei*, 35 ; *De Natura Boni
contra Manichaeos*, 4 ; *De diversis Quaestionibus*, 83, q. 6.

[21] Noli foras ire, in teipsum redi ; in interiori
homine habitat veritas. (*De Vera Religione*, 39.)

[22] Deum et animam scire cupis. Nihilne plus ?
Nihil omnino. (*Soliloq.* 1, 2.)

[23] Itaque confundebar et convertebar et gaudebam,
Deus meus, quod ecclesia unica, corpus Unici tui,
in qua mihi nomen Christi infanti est inditum, non
saperet infantiles nugas. (*Conf.* vi, 4 ; cf. vii, 1.)

[24] In ictu trepidantis aspectus. (*Ibid.*, vii, 17.)

[25] *Ibid.*, vi, 11.

[26] Quam tibi sordidus, quam foedus, quam
exsecrabilis, quam horribilis complexus femineus
videbatur, quando inter nos de uxoris cupiditate
quaesitum est. (*Soliloq.* 1, 14 ; cf. 1, 10.)

[27] *Conf.*, vi, 12.

[28] Ita duae voluntates meae, una vetus, alia nova, illa
carnalis, illa spiritalis, confligebant inter se atque
discordando dissipabant animam meam. (*Ibid.*, viii, 5.)

[29] *Ibid.*, vii, 12.

[30] *Ibid.*, v, 10.

[31] *Ibid.*, vii, 19.

[32] *De Ordine*, 1, 10.

[33] Itaque si hanc vitam illi viri nobiscum rursum
agere potuissent, viderent profecto cujus auctoritate
facilius consuleretur hominibus et paucis mutatis
verbis atque sententiis Christiani fierent, sicut plerique
recentiorum nostrorumque temporum Platonici fecerunt.

(*De Vera Religione*, 4 ; cf. *Contra Academicos*, III, 20; *De Civitate Dei*, VIII, 4.)

[34] Est enim species prima, qua sunt, ut ita dicam, speciata, et forma qua formata sunt omnia. (*De div. Quaest.* 83, q. 23.)

[35] Religet ergo nos religio uni omnipotenti Deo ; quia inter mentem nostram, qua illum intelligimus Patrem, et Veritatem, i.e., lucem interiorem, per quam illum intelligimus, nulla interposita creatura est. Quare ipsam quoque Veritatem nulla ex parte dissimilem in ipso et cum ipso veneremur, quae forma est omnium, quae ab uno facta sunt et ad unum nituntur. Unde apparet spiritalibus animis, per hanc formam esse facta omnia, quae sola implet, quod appetunt omnia. (*De Vera Religione*, 55 ; cf. *De Magistro*, 11 ; *De Moribus Eccl.*, 1, 17 ; *De div. Quaest.* 83, qq. 46, 54.)

[36] Trinitas . . . ita etiam a paucis sanctis beatisque intelligitur. (*Epistola* XI, 2 ; cf. *De Vera Religione*, 7.)

[37] *De Quantitate Animae*, 33 ; *De Vera Religione*, 26.

[38] *De Vera Religione*, 5.

[39] Quid est aliud beate vivere nisi aeternum aliquid cognoscendo habere (*De div. Quaest.* 83, q. 35) ; in tantum enim est beatitudo nostra in quantum ejus (sc. Domini) contemplatione perfruimur (q. 69).

[40] *De Utilitate Credendi*, 12, 16.

[41] *De Magistro*, 11.

[42] *Contra Academicos*, III, 19.

[43] *De Vera Religione*, 16 ; *Epistola* XI, 4 ; *De div. Quaest.* 83, qq. 36 et 43.

[44] *De Utilitate Credendi*, 14 ; *De div. Quaest.* 83, q. 25.

[45] Debeo scripturarum ejus medicamenta omnia perscrutari (Ep. XXI, 3.).

[46] Whether of its own reflective effort, or by borrowing from Jeremias. *De Doctrina Christiana* II, 28; *De Civitate Dei*, VIII, 11.

[47] *Retractationes* I, 1.

[48] *Ibid.*, I, 3.

[49] *Ibid.*, I, 4; I, 1.

[50] *De Civitate Dei*, XIX, 25; cf. V, 12; *Contra Julianum*, IV, 3.

[51] Quid est ergo credere in eum? Credendo amare, credendo diligere, credendo in eum ire et ejus membris incorporari. (*In Joannem*, XXIX, 6.)

[52] *Epistola* LV, 10.

[53] Dilige, et quod vis fac. (*In Epistolam Joannis*, VII, 8.)

[54] *Ibid.*, V, 7.

[55] *De div. Quaest.* 83, q. 68.

[56] *Contra Fortunatum*, 16; De Libero Arbitrio, III, 19, 20, 22.

[57] Cf. *Expositio quar. prop.*, 44.

[58] *De Praedest. Sanct.*, 3, 4; *Retract.*, I, 23.

[59] *De div. Quaest. ad Simplicianum*, I, 2; cf. *De Praedest. Sanct.*, 3.

[60] Sunt omnes homines . . . una quaedam massa peccati. *De div. Quaest. ad Simpl.*, I, 2; cf. *De Gratia et Peccato Orig.*, 2, 39.

[61] *Sermo* CXLIV, 5; *Enarrat. in Ps.* XXVII, 2; CXC, 2; LVI, 5; *Sermo* CXXVI, 6.

[62] Ecclesiae principium et primitiae. (*In Ep. Joannis*, II, 2.)

[63] *Ibid.*, I, 2.

[64] *Sermo* CXLIV, 5 ; XLV, 4 ; *In Joannem*, XXI, 8.

[65] Cf. *De Doctrina Christiana*, III, 42-55.

[66] Cf. *Epist.* CLXVI, 3.

[67] *Retract.*, I, 10.

[68] *De Vera Religione*, 27.

[69] *Enarr. in Ps.* LXII, 2.

[70] *Enarr. in Ps.* LXXXIV, 13.

[71] *Enarr. in Ps.* CXXIX, 7.

[72] Cf. *De Natura et Gratia*, 2 ; *In Joannem*, VIII, 4.

[73] Ipsa quoque noſtra juſtitia, quamvis vera sit propter veri boni finem, ad quem refertur, tamen tanta eſt in hac vita, ut potius peccatorum remissione conſtet quam perfeƈtione virtutum. (*De Civitate Dei*, XIX, 27.)

[74] Non ergo quia futuri eramus (sancti), sed ut essemus. (*De Praedest. Sanctorum*, 18 ; cf. *De Correptione et Gratia*, 7 ; *Epist.* CLXXXVI, 7.)

[75] Proinde posse habere fidem sicut posse habere caritatem, naturae eſt hominum ; habere autem fidem quemadmodum habere caritatem, gratiae eſt fidelium. Illa itaque natura, in qua nobis data eſt possibilitas habendi fidem, non discernit ab homine hominem. Ipsa vero fides discernit ab infideli fidelem. (*De Praedest. Sanctorum*, 5.)

[76] Nemo habet in poteſtate, quid ei veniat in mentem, sed consentire vel dissentire propriae voluntatis eſt. (*De Spiritu et Littera*, 34.)

[77] Ipsa suavitas te trahit. (*Sermo* CXXXI, 2.)

[78] Haec enim voluntas libera tanto erit liberior, quanto sanior, tanto autem sanior, quanto divinae

misericordiae gratiaeque subjectior. (*Epist.* CLVII, 2 ; cf. *Sermo* CLV, 3.)

[79] Subventum est igitur infirmitati voluntatis humanae, ut divina gratia indeclinabiliter et insuperabiliter ageretur, et ideo, quamvis infirma, non tamen deficeret neque adversitate aliqua vinceretur. (*De Correptione et Gratia*, 12.)

[80] Profecto et ipsum velle credere Deus operatur in homine et in omnibus misericordia ejus praevenit nos. (*De Spiritu et Littera*, 34.)

[81] *Enarr. in Ps.* CXXX, 14.

[82] Et erit unus Christus amans seipsum. (*In Epist. Joannis*, X, 3.)

[83] Mundus damnatus, quidquid praeter Ecclesiam ; mundus reconciliatus, Ecclesia. (*Sermo* XCVI, 8 ; cf. *Epist.* CLXXXV, 50.)

[84] Origo mea Christus est, radix mea Christus est, caput meum Christus est. (*Contra Litteras Petiliani*, I, 7.)

A MONUMENT
TO
ST. AUGUSTINE

*ESSAYS ON HIS AGE,
LIFE, AND THOUGHT*

BY

M. C. D'ARCY, S. J., MAURICE
BLONDEL, CHRISTOPHER DAWSON,
ETIENNE GILSON, JACQUES
MARITAIN, C.C. MARTINDALE, S.J.,
ERICH PRZYWARA, S.J. JOHN-
BAPTIST REEVES, O.P., B. ROLAND-
GOSSELIN, E. I. WATKIN.

Demy 8vo. 368 pp. 12s. 6d. net

"A remarkable tribute."—*New Statesman.*

"Sympathetic and inspiring commemoration."
Sunday Times.

"No more appropriate monument could have
been devised."—*Observer.*

"Admirable . . . attractive . . brilliant."
Spectator.

KARL ADAM

CHRIST OUR BROTHER

Cr. 8vo.   210 pp.   7s. 6d. net.

" The best of the three volumes (Karl Adam)
has given us. (He has an) extraordinary gift for
catching the soul of a thing."—ARCHBISHOP GOODIER,
Clergy Review.

THE SPIRIT
OF CATHOLICISM

Cr. 8vo.   270 pp.   3s. 6d. net.

"No one can say he has thoroughly sounded
the depths of the Roman problem who has not read
it."—*Review of the Churches*

"A most complete and alluring study of the
beauty of the Catholic faith."
Church of England Newspaper.

CHRIST
AND THE WESTERN MIND :
LOVE AND BELIEF
TWO ESSAYS

Cr. 8vo.   80 pp.   3s. 6d. net.

"Both essays are tremendously powerful ; every
sentence is arresting."—*Universe*

"Alert ... active ... sensitive ... utterly alive."
Dublin Review.

ERICH PRZYWARA, S.J.

A NEWMAN
SYNTHESIS

PASSAGES TAKEN FROM EVERY PART
OF HIS WRITINGS AND ARRANGED AS
A CONTINUOUS TREATISE

Large Cr.   380 pp.   7s. 6d. net.

" This single volume separates what is permanent
from what was merely of its own time in a score of
volumes.   But it is not an anthology.   It is a
systematic presentation of Newman's thought, in
his own language, beginning with the idea of God,
and marking out, through a hundred stages, the
whole upward journey of the soul."—ALFRED NOYES
in *The Sunday Times.*

" The pith of Newman . . . will appeal to many
who quail before the immensity of his works and
are yet anxious to compass his religious teaching
and its application."—*Observer.*

" A masterly analysis."—*Dublin Review.*

JACQUES   CHEVALIER

PASCAL

Demy 8vo.   336 pp.   15s. net.

" Every schoolboy, in the notorious Macaulayan
phrase is presumed to know his Pascal, but actually
there is strangely little about him in English.
Perhaps the lack of a first-rate biography is one
reason for the neglect, but this can no longer be
pleaded in excuse.   M. Chevalier not only makes
the man but the time and the Port-Royal controversy live again.   An admirable piece of work."
Saturday Review.